PIANO SOLO

CONTEMPORARY
HYMN
Stylings

ARRANGED BY MARIANNE KIM

T0065947

ISBN 978-1-4803-6101-0

SHAWNEE PRESS

EXCLUSIVELY DISTRIBUTED BY

HAL•LEONARD®

Visit Hal Leonard Online at
www.halleonard.com

Visit Shawnee Press Online at
www.shawneepress.com

Contact Us:
Hal Leonard
7777 West Bluemound Road
Milwaukee, WI 53213
Email: info@halleonard.com

In Europe contact:
Hal Leonard Europe Limited
Distribution Centre, Newmarket Road
Bury St Edmunds, Suffolk, IP33 3YB
Email: info@halleonardeurope.com

In Australia contact:
Hal Leonard Australia Pty. Ltd.
4 Lentara Court
Cheltenham, Victoria, 3192 Australia
Email: info@halleonard.com.au

FOREWORD

In this collection, Marianne Kim adds her special touch to time-honored songs of the faith. With purity of purpose and thoughtful craftsmanship, she finds the sacred in every chord. She treads softly with sensitive care, never losing the essence of the hymns, and the result is an elegant variety of pieces well-suited for sanctuary usage. The smooth, fresh sounds of these selections are gentle on the ear and enriching to the soul.

– Joseph M. Martin

I first met Marianne Kim in December 2000 when she came to Kansas City for a consultation and piano lesson with me. I was impressed with her talent at the keyboard and her passion to learn. Since that time, we've stayed in contact and I've watched her grow into an amazing composer, arranger, accompanist and studio musician. As a pianist, she plays all styles, and what she doesn't know, she learns. There is a rich well of creativity within Marianne. She is a bright new talent on the Christian music scene and I expect her to make a great contribution to church music.

– Mark Hayes

ABOUT THE ARRANGER

Marianne Kim (b. 1972) is a Chicago-based composer, arranger, pianist, organist and harpsichordist. She has been noted for her vibrant performances and compositions in a wide diversity of sacred and secular musical styles. As a soloist and collaborative artist, Marianne enjoys performing piano and organ recitals, chamber music and jazz. She has served as keyboardist for the Lakeside Singers, Willow Creek Community Church and the Moody Church. Her music has been published through The Lorenz Corporation, Hope Publishing, Augsburg Fortress, Yesol Publishing Company (Korea) and Shawnee Press/Hal Leonard.

CONTENTS

DOWN AT THE CROSS
(Glory to His Name)

Arranged by
MARIANNE KIM

Words by ELISHA A. HOFFMAN
Music by JOHN H. STOCKTON

I WILL SING OF MY REDEEMER

Arranged by
MARIANNE KIM

Words by PHILIP P. BLISS
Music by JAMES McGRANAHAN

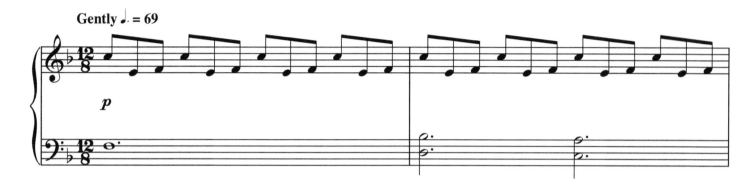

JESUS PAID IT ALL

Arranged by
MARIANNE KIM

Words by ELVINA M. HALL
Music by JOHN T. GRAPE

LET US BREAK BREAD TOGETHER

Arranged by
MARIANNE KIM

Traditional Spiritual

NEAR TO THE HEART OF GOD

Arranged by
MARIANNE KIM

Words and Music by
CLELAND B. McAFEE

SAVIOR, LIKE A SHEPHERD LEAD US

Arranged by
MARIANNE KIM

Words from *Hymns For The Young*
Attributed to DOROTHY A. THRUPP
Music by WILLIAM B. BRADBURY

Flowing ♩ = 108

SOFTLY AND TENDERLY

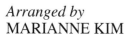

Arranged by
MARIANNE KIM

Words and Music by
WILL L. THOMPSON

STAND UP, STAND UP FOR JESUS

Arranged by
MARIANNE KIM

Words by GEORGE DUFFIELD, JR.
Music by GEORGE J. WEBB

TRUSTING JESUS

Arranged by
MARIANNE KIM

Words by EDGAR PAGE STITES
Music by IRA D. SANKEY

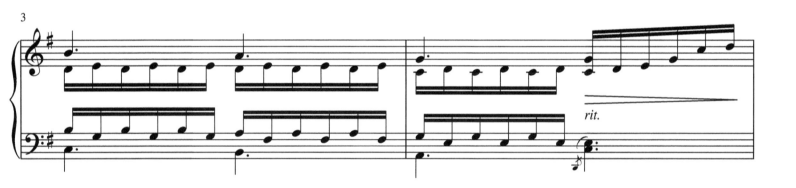

WHAT A FRIEND WE HAVE IN JESUS

Arranged by
MARIANNE KIM

Words by JOSEPH M. SCRIVEN
Music by CHARLES C. CONVERSE

PIANO & ORGAN COLLECTIONS
from Shawnee Press

BEGINNING ORGANIST – VOLUME 1
by Darwin Wolford
Each piece is carefully edited, complete with fingerings and pedal indications, making it an excellent teaching resource. Includes: "Duet" by Handel, "From Heaven on High" by Reger, "Voluntary" by Boellmann, "Andante" by Zollner, and "In Dulci Jubilo" by Bach.
_____ 35001866 Organ Solo $14.99

FIFTEEN PIECES FOR CHURCH OR RECITAL
by Gordon Young
Includes: Air • Antiphon • Bachiana • Benedictus • Canzona • Concertino • Divertissement • Glorificamus • Marche • Offertorium • Postludium • Prelude on "Blessed Assurance" • Toccata • Trumpet Gigue • Trumpet Voluntary.
_____ 35006677 Organ Solo $19.99

GO OUT IN JOY – FESTIVE POSTLUDES FOR PIANO
A variety of styles and difficulty levels are included, with careful attention paid to choose hymns that have the spirit of celebration in both tune and text. Enjoy the work of Vicki Tucker Courtney, Cindy Berry, Brad Nix, Alex-Zsolt, Hojun Lee and others!
_____ 35028092 Piano Solo $16.99

GOSPEL GOLD
Featuring Arrangements from: Cindy Berry, Patti Drennan, Mark Hayes, Lloyd Larson, and others
Some of today's best pianists and arrangers have gathered to celebrate the best timeless gospel hymns in a new compilation sure to be a hit with any church pianist. 17 songs, including: Stand Up, Stand Up for Jesus • 'Tis So Sweet to Trust in Jesus • Just a Closer Walk with Thee • Do Lord • Rock of Ages • He Keeps Me Singing • and many more.
_____ 35027306 Piano Solo $16.99

GOSPEL GOLD – VOLUME 2
Stretch your offertory options with this brilliant collection from some of today's most respected piano arrangers: Mary McDonald, Pamela Robertson, Shirley Brendlinger, Brad Nix, James Koerts, Carolyn Hamlin and others.
_____ 35028093 Piano Solo $16.99

HYMNS OF GRATEFUL PRAISE
arr. Lee Dengler
Includes: For the Beauty of the Earth • Joyful, Joyful We Adore Thee • Morning Has Broken • Fairest Lord Jesus • Now Thank We All Our God • Holy God We Praise Thy Name • All Creatures of Our God and King • Praise to the Lord the Almighty • Praise Him! Praise Him! • and more.
_____ 35028339 Piano Solo $16.99

IMAGES
arr. Heather Sorenson
When combined with the innovative visual supplement, the church pianist moves their ministry from its traditional role into a new area of expression. Includes: Beautiful • I Surrender All • Fairest Lord Jesus • Blest Be the Tie • I Must Tell Jesus • It Is Well • Brethren We Have Met to Worship • Whiter Than Snow • A Mighty Fortress • The Journey (with He Leadeth Me).
_____ 35028265 Piano Solo $16.99
_____ 35028266 Listening CD $16.99
_____ 35028277 Piano Solos Book/
                            DVD-ROM Pack $29.99

JOY TO THE WORLD
arr. Jack Jones
Includes: Joy to the World • Angels We Have Heard on High • Coventry Carol • Deck the Hall • Ding Dong! Merrily on High! • Good Christians, All Rejoice • Good People All This Christmas Time • Infant Holy, Infant Lowly • Rise Up, Shepherd, and Follow.
_____ 35028373 Organ Solo $16.99

MUSIC OF THE MASTERS FOR THE MASTER
Using a classical theme or genre as the basis for each piece, the composer weds a time-honored hymn to bring these beloved themes into the sanctuary. Included in this thoughtful assembly is the writing of Mary McDonald, Cindy Berry, Carolyn Hamlin, Joseph Martin, Alex-Zsolt, Jack Jones, James Michael Stevens and many others.
_____ 35028091 Piano Solo $19.99

SIMPLY BEAUTIFUL
Includes: What a Friend We Have in Jesus • Be Thou My Vision • Tis So Sweet to Trust In Jesus • I Am Bound for the Promised Land • Shades of Dawn • Softly and Tenderly • I Am His and He Is Mine • Jesus Keep Me Near the Cross • Shall We Gather At the River • and many more.
_____ 35027735 Piano Solo $16.95

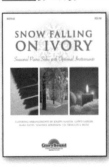

SNOW FALLING ON IVORY
From tender carols of reflections to sparkling songs of joy, this collection has something for everybody. Includes: Dance at the Manger • Ding Dong Merrily on High • Gesu Bambino • Go, Tell It on the Mountain • In the Bleak Mid-Winter • It Came Upon a Midnight Clear • Let All Mortal Flesh Keep Silence • and more.
_____ 35020710 Piano Solo $24.95

SNOW FALLING ON IVORY – VOLUME 2
Pianists may play the arrangements as piano solos or perform them in tandem with the optional instrumental descants for something truly special. Arrangers include: Joseph Martin, John Purifoy, Lee Dengler, Vicki Tucker Courtney, Brad Nix, Harry Strack, Matt Hyzer, Shirley Brendlinger, Alex-Zsolt, James Koerts and Joel Raney.
_____ 35028386 Piano Solo $19.99

EXCLUSIVELY DISTRIBUTED BY

Prices, contents, and availability subject to change without notice.

0413

The Best
Sacred Collections
for Piano

Blended Worship Piano Collection

Songs include: Amazing Grace (My Chains Are Gone) • Be Thou My Vision • I Will Rise • Joyful, Joyful, We Adore Thee • Lamb of God • Majesty • Open the Eyes of My Heart • Praise to the Lord, the Almighty • Shout to the Lord • 10,000 Reasons (Bless the Lord) • Worthy Is the Lamb • Your Name • and more.
00293528 Piano Solo $17.99

Hymn Anthology

A beautiful collection of 60 hymns arranged for piano solo, including: Abide with Me • Be Thou My Vision • Come, Thou Fount of Every Blessing • Doxology • For the Beauty of the Earth • God of Grace and God of Glory • Holy, Holy, Holy • It Is Well with My Soul • Joyful, Joyful, We Adore Thee • Let Us Break Bread Together • A Mighty Fortress Is Our God • O God, Our Help in Ages Past • Savior, like a Shepherd Lead Us • To God Be the Glory • What a Friend We Have in Jesus • and more.
00251244 Piano Solo $16.99

The Hymn Collection

arranged by Phillip Keveren

17 beloved hymns expertly and beautifully arranged for solo piano by Phillip Keveren. Includes: All Hail the Power of Jesus' Name • I Love to Tell the Story • I Surrender All • I've Got Peace Like a River • Were You There? • and more.
00311071 Piano Solo $14.99

Hymn Duets

arranged by Phillip Keveren

Includes lovely duet arrangements of: All Creatures of Our God and King • I Surrender All • It Is Well with My Soul • O Sacred Head, Now Wounded • Praise to the Lord, The Almighty • Rejoice, The Lord Is King • and more.
00311544 Piano Duet..$14.99

Hymn Medleys

arranged by Phillip Keveren

Great medleys resonate with the human spirit, as do the truths in these moving hymns. Here Phillip Keveren combines 24 timeless favorites into eight lovely medleys for solo piano.
00311349 Piano Solo $14.99

P/V/G = Piano/Vocal/Guitar arrangements.

Prices, contents and availability subject to change without notice.

Hymns for Two

arranged by Carol Klose

12 piano duet arrangements of favorite hymns: Amazing Grace • Be Thou My Vision • Crown Him with Many Crowns • Fairest Lord Jesus • Holy, Holy, Holy • I Need Thee Every Hour • O Worship the King • What a Friend We Have in Jesus • and more.
00290544 Piano Duet..$12.99

It Is Well
10 BELOVED HYMNS FOR MEMORIAL SERVICES
arr. John Purifoy

10 peaceful, soul-stirring hymn settings appropriate for memorial services and general worship use. Titles include: Abide with Me • Amazing Grace • Be Still My Soul • For All the Saints • His Eye Is on the Sparrow • In the Garden • It Is Well with My Soul • Like a River Glorious • Rock of Ages • What a Friend We Have in Jesus.
00118920 Piano Solo $12.99

Ragtime Gospel Classics

arr. Steven K. Tedesco

A dozen old-time gospel favorites: Because He Lives • Goodbye World Goodbye • He Touched Me • I Saw the Light • I'll Fly Away • Keep on the Firing Line • Mansion over the Hilltop • No One Ever Cared for Me like Jesus • There Will Be Peace in the Valley for Me • Victory in Jesus • What a Day That Will Be • Where Could I Go.
00142449 Piano Solo $11.99

Ragtime Gospel Hymns

arranged by Steven Tedesco

15 traditional gospel hymns, including: At Calvary • Footsteps of Jesus • Just a Closer Walk with Thee • Leaning on the Everlasting Arms • What a Friend We Have in Jesus • When We All Get to Heaven • and more.
00311763 Piano Solo $10.99

Sacred Classics for Solo Piano

arr. John Purifoy

10 timeless songs of faith, masterfully arranged by John Purifoy. Because He Lives • Easter Song • Glorify Thy Name • Here Am I, Send Me • I'd Rather Have Jesus • Majesty • On Eagle's Wings • There's Something About That Name • We Shall Behold Him • Worthy Is the Lamb.
00141703 Piano Solo $14.99

Raise Your Hands
PIANO SOLOS FOR BLENDED WORSHIP
arr. Heather Sorenson

10 uplifting and worshipful solos crafted by Heather Sorenson. Come Thou Fount, Come Thou King • God of Heaven • Holy Is the Lord (with "Holy, Holy, Holy") • Holy Spirit • I Will Rise • In Christ Alone • Raise Your Hands • Revelation Song • 10,000 Reasons (Bless the Lord) • Your Name (with "All Hail the Power of Jesus' Name").
00231579 Piano Solo $14.99

Seasonal Sunday Solos for Piano

24 blended selections grouped by occasion. Includes: Breath of Heaven (Mary's Song) • Come, Ye Thankful People, Come • Do You Hear What I Hear • God of Our Fathers • In the Name of the Lord • Mary, Did You Know? • Mighty to Save • Spirit of the Living God • The Wonderful Cross • and more.
00311971 Piano Solo $16.99

Sunday Solos for Piano

30 blended selections, perfect for the church pianist. Songs include: All Hail the Power of Jesus' Name • Be Thou My Vision • Great Is the Lord • Here I Am to Worship • Majesty • Open the Eyes of My Heart • and many more.
00311272 Piano Solo $17.99

More Sunday Solos for Piano

A follow-up to *Sunday Solos for Piano*, this collection features 30 more blended selections perfect for the church pianist. Includes: Agnus Dei • Come, Thou Fount of Every Blessing • The Heart of Worship • How Great Thou Art • Immortal, Invisible • O Worship the King • Shout to the Lord • Thy Word • We Fall Down • and more.
00311864 Piano Solo $16.99

Even More Sunday Solos for Piano

30 blended selections, including: Ancient Words • Brethren, We Have Met to Worship • How Great Is Our God • Lead On, O King Eternal • Offering • Savior, Like a Shepherd Lead Us • We Bow Down • Worthy of Worship • and more.
00312098 Piano Solo $16.99